MW01135327

Guide t(Needs Assessment for Integrated Information Resource Management and Collection Development

edited by
Dora Biblarz
Stephen Bosch
Chris Sugnet

Collection Management and Development Guides, No. 11
Association for Library Collections & Technical Services
A Division of the American Library Association

The Scarecrow Press, Inc.
Lanham, Maryland, and London
2001

SCARECROW PRESS, INC.

Published in the United States of America
by Scarecrow Press, Inc.
A wholly owned subsidiary of The Rowman & Littlefield Publishing Group, Inc.
4501 Forbes Blvd., Suite 200, Lanham, Maryland 20706
www.scarecrowpress.com

Copyright © 2001 by the American Library Association
Guide developed for: American Library Association, Association for
Library Collections and Technical Services, Collection Management and
Development Section, Collection Development Issues for the Practitioner
Committee

Library of Congress Cataloging-in-Publication Data

Guide to library user needs assessment for integrated information resource management and
collection development / edited by Dora Biblarz, Stephen Bosch, Chris Sugnet
    p. cm.—(Collection management and development guides ; no. 11)
"Association for Library Collections and Technical Services, a division of the American Library
Association"
Includes bibliographical references.
    ISBN 0-8108-4131-2 (alk. paper)
    1. Collection management (Libraries). 2. Library use studies. 3. Needs assessment. I.
Biblarz, Dora. II. Bosch, Stephen. III. Sugnet, Chris. IV. Association for Library Collections &
Technical Services. V. Series.
    Z687 .G847 2001
    025.58—dc21

                                                                    2001031447

Contents

Introduction

This guide is intended to examine the practice, benefits, and specific methods for assessing library users' information needs in any type of library.

In this context, needs assessment refers to a process of using one or more techniques to collect and analyze data regarding library users or potential users. Specifically, the data collected will be directly or indirectly related to the needs, in the broadest sense, of users, or customers, for information in all formats. Interpretation of the data will influence the management of collections, including such options as offering electronic full-text and rapid document delivery services.

The scope of this guide includes the methodology and techniques for carrying out needs assessment projects, ranging from short-term assessments to long-term research or comprehensive collection assessments. The types of data, techniques, and methodology are described, as are associated pointers and pitfalls.

I. The reasons for undertaking needs assessment, defining the value of user assessments, and the theory concerning user needs assessment

The data collection and analysis of user needs is part of a larger strategy within the library under the responsibility of collection development personnel—that of collection management—and it falls into the broad, librarywide planning process. Information concerning the needs of library users should impact policies and procedures in all aspects of library services. In the context of designing and providing services that are based on the defined needs of users (instead of the needs librarians have traditionally attributed to users) and improvements that are based on user satisfaction, needs assessment takes on a high priority. Although collection managers have carried out needs assessment projects in the past, their efforts have been directed to long-term needs for future use, working toward building research or comprehensive-level collections over decades and generations, more than for present or short-term needs. The implication that needs assessment can also help plan and offer "just-in-time" solutions is innovative. Few libraries can continue to build in-depth collections, hoping the collections will be used sometime in the future.

Collection managers are accustomed to being held accountable for the way the materials budget is allocated and expended. What is new and different is that accountability can be measured from a variety of perspectives. In fact, the statistical results that were held in high regard in the past (e.g., the library added 120 new titles in subject area x last year) are now in question, and those questions that must be asked might include, "Are those titles the most effective 120 new titles that could have been purchased? How can we determine that these titles are the most effective? How do these titles satisfy the needs of the library's users?" Efficiency, effectiveness, or performance measures are being designed and used to evaluate the success of outcomes of library programs that aim to support a variety of information needs, including research, education (continuing, remedial, distance, etc.), leisure reading, business, or hobby. As user satisfaction is added to the list of measurable outcomes that are used to evaluate the success of goals and objectives, libraries will seek new methods to measure actual need and demonstrate satisfaction with their services.

The proliferation of electronic resources and Web access has exerted such influence over the information needs of library users that the paradigms of print/nonprint, or monograph/serial, need to be reframed. Former paradigms should be enhanced by such choices as: "Do you want the article faxed to your office within twenty-four hours or will you pick it up?" and "Are you on campus/in town or using our system remotely?" Within this concept, information needs can be filled by many methods—some, but not all, of which lead to the development of the collection in the traditional sense. Integrated information needs assessment addresses the full range of options available to satisfy library user needs at the beginning of the twenty-first century.

In some form or other, the mission statement of almost every academic library claims to support the curricular and research activities of the students and faculty. Public libraries base their mission on the needs of the community. Libraries with special foci are generally closely linked in mission to their parent organization, again, focusing their support as closely as possible on the research and information needs of their constituency. Every type of library should have formal collection development policies that declare its specific mission, the scope of the collection, and areas of strength or weakness; in addition, the policies should indicate, in some form, plans for future development. With the use of needs assessment as well as other assessment strategies, the library can illustrate and defend the collection choices it has made in a responsible manner.

Many libraries invite their users' help in building the collection directly by making suggestions for individual titles or materials in special interest areas, or indirectly by demanding "hot" titles or best sellers. Public libraries also seek information by examining trends in their communities—e.g., a popular talk show host who selects a book for the focus of the day's discussion will generate interest in that title from a certain segment of the community. Many then go to their public library to look for the item.

In research and academic institutions, librarians with subject assignments typically set up a communication system with faculty in the areas of their responsibility. Armed with the syllabi and reading lists for courses and seminars, the librarians then use these as resources for building the collection to support the academic program. If all goes well, relationships develop that lead to focused development in areas of the faculty members' research, if the faculty's interests are within the scope of the libraries'/institutions' interests. Some institutions depend on the selection activities of faculty, a classical paradigm; others rely on various combinations of faculty selection, librarian selection, blanket orders, and approval plans. Interested and vocal individuals seldom hesitate to notify librarians of their needs. Less vocal users may not vocalize their needs. It is important for librarians to let faculty know that their requests for library materials will be taken seriously.

Beginning in the 1980s, when the serious escalation of serial prices kept eroding the base budget for library materials, libraries took radical steps to realign priorities and serial cancellation projects became annual or semiannual events. This new pressure on the materials budget has had the unexpected benefit of focusing critical evaluations on collections and the materials' usefulness to today's patrons. Studies of the use of circulating collections seemed cumbersome and time-consuming, even with the assistance of automated systems. Staff, already busy reshelving a heavily used collection, resisted additional work involved with the study of the use of noncirculating collections, such as current issues of periodicals. But data from use studies, including academic faculty surveys for the review of serials, used with other criteria, can provide essential information to determine priorities for retention and cancellation decisions. Even though there may be methodological problems with most periodical use studies, these studies over time do provide useful data that can be combined with other data-collecting techniques to eventually form a balanced picture of the use of the collection. There are drawbacks. For example, when the single act of reshelving a title is counted as one use, the issues are counted even when some patrons simply pull the issues of a favorite title off the shelf and do not actually use them; when patrons put used items back on the shelf and do not actually use them, the use of the item is not counted; or multiple uses of an item occur before it is reshelved, and these uses are missed in the count.

Designing collection management strategies around user needs has not been done in a consistent, systematic manner in the past. Academic faculty may engage in selection activities, but not all faculty will be involved and their level of involvement is not consistent over long periods of time. User suggestions may be solicited but perhaps not acted upon in a consistent manner or not treated uniformly by all selectors. Another problem may be that the user request involves unrealistic expectations—for instance, very rare or expensive materials are requested for general circulating collections, or academic libraries may receive inappropriate requests for subscriptions not within the purchasing scope of the institution. The harried library patron who is looking for immediate resources may be the most difficult to satisfy, as those patrons sometimes expect that specific information will be made available to them within an unrealistic time frame (immediately).

Today, with the proliferation of electronic resources, which provide full-text articles from periodicals online or via CD-ROM, fax delivery within a few hours of identification from commercial services, cooperative network agreements that provide twenty-four-hour (or shorter) turnaround on interlibrary loan (ILL) requests, etc., libraries can satisfy the needs of patrons in new ways without having to own the physical materials. These services satisfy user needs, and the services reflect collection management decisions including resource-sharing agreements, contracts for commercial services, and reliance on electronic resources—all selected with short-term needs of the clientele as top priority.

Needs assessment is a category within the client-centered series of techniques and tools that can be used by libraries to refine and improve services with demonstrable outcomes. Guided by a combination of technological expertise and the results of needs assessments, as well as other tools, libraries can provide information services in a responsible manner, justifying changes based on real data, not just impressions or intuitive feelings.

Other factors are also focusing pressure on libraries. Competition for users as well as for resources forces the improvement of existing services and the creation of more innovative services aimed toward user satisfaction. For example, previous assumptions that libraries will continue to be funded based on their implicit cultural advantages have been tested lately, and the results have not been positive. Libraries can no longer take for granted that they will always be a dynamic part of any community or organization. The need to be accountable to funding agencies creates an environment in which performance measures must be used to demonstrate success. Using data from user satisfaction surveys can help demonstrate accountability.

The growth of competition between libraries and commercial document delivery services or the growth of competition between libraries and copy shops selling course-packs (reserve reading lists) are examples of the phenomena of other organizations providing new services because user demands were not adequately satisfied by libraries. The ease and availability of access have been aided by technology to which the private sector has added the entrepreneurial spirit—and that makes it possible to fill this need at a profit. If this approach is more convenient and saves time and frustration, users will pursue it as an alternative to libraries. The fact that information costs money is not viewed as a deterrent. The growth of competing services raises several questions. What information services are central to the success of libraries? Which services are best outsourced? Which services should be left to the private sector?

Technological innovations make many types of information accessible in ways never addressed by traditional library services. In the area of distance learning, offering courses at locations distant from the main campus via the Internet and teleconferencing are obvious examples. Traditional academic institutions are discovering a need to compete with institutions that offer degree programs or individual courses on weekends or during the evenings, at the job location, or through other options including instructional television or distance learning technology. While the traditional library ponders how to support these nontraditional, geographically dispersed classes with books and readings from the collection, placing the materials on reserve at nearby public or college libraries, instructors are bypassing the library, creating reading lists and having course-packs and related materials assembled or digitized by copy shops or educational software providers.

When is the appropriate time to undertake information-related needs assessment projects? There is no specific time. As many library information services are being developed with the short-term needs of the patron in mind, the need to know which resources are most needed becomes crucial. In most libraries, the support of new programs, new user groups, or new directions in research, especially when no new sources of funds are available, requires a reallocation of existing resources. User needs assessments are an excellent way to focus limited funds into realistic collection or resource building.

For some libraries, the strategic planning process illuminates new directions for collection priorities. No longer in a constant mode of building and growing collections, the collection manager today is also forced to cap collecting programs to develop other areas, cancel subscriptions to journals, and withdraw materials that no longer fit the collections' guidelines. Assessments are crucial for discovering needs that did not exist or were not previously known, and for managing user expectations under circumstances where budgets are static and purchasing power continues to decline. Assessments are also helpful in verifying the decline in use in areas of the collection that have been heavily used in the past.

Library organizations and the collections that libraries strive to manage should represent dynamic systems that grow and change, so they remain viable and interesting even as conditions change in the society around them. Collection managers in all types of libraries should constantly seek feedback on the results of their efforts and try out new approaches to service that demonstrate their indispensable nature to the community. Reductions in programs or the materials budget need to be translated into efficient changes in collection strategies.

The community of users will constantly change and grow, or shrink in some areas, whether it is an academic, public, or specialized library. In the private sector, mergers and buyouts can create sudden changes in the mission and scope of the parent organization, and these changes cascade down to all parts, including the library. Taking user needs into consideration when planning services, budgeting, or implementing reductions is vital for continued success in any service organization, whether it be in the public or for-profit arena.

The direct benefits of undertaking user needs assessments for collection development and management uses can include:

- Maximizing the potential of programs, collections, and services to support user needs.
- Providing data that assists in the allocation of resources.
- Providing data that supports program planning.
- Providing verifiable justification for requesting new resources.
- Supporting the development of verifiable performance and quality measures.
- Ensuring that resources are serving the clientele's/users' objectives.
- Supporting strategies that combine access and ownership to provide the best service.
- Providing justification for reducing collecting activities in subject areas where materials are not heavily used.

There are some caveats to the issue of conducting information needs assessments. Depending on the project's scope, significant resources may be required in terms of staff time, materials (forms, etc.), costs for consultants, or costs for software and related processing. Another aspect to be aware of is the tendency for findings to meet expectations. In other words, by examining a certain issue, one is proceeding on the assumption that the issue merits the scrutiny. Caution must be exercised to avoid anticipating the results and designing a study focused solely to look for expected or desired results. There are cost/benefit issues also: the expected outcomes of the project should be weighed in terms of the cost of doing the assessment. Some fine-tuning may be necessary so that the work done on the assessment corresponds with the expected outcomes/ learnings. The assessment can be expensive but still worth doing, and it may be worthwhile doing some redesign to cut costs, or allocating additional funds if the outcome is viewed as central to strategic interests of the organization.

II. The process for developing a needs assessment project

A. Establish the goals of the assessment

It is important to clearly define the goals of the project. What aspects of your users' information needs do you need to measure? As outlined in the previous section, several types of projects could require an assessment of users' needs. Projects will vary in the types of data needed to achieve expected outcomes. Expected outcomes need to be explicitly defined. Are the outcomes worth the resources allocated to the project? Is there a path to integrate assessment results into decision-making processes? An important aspect of goal setting includes reviewing the organization's political environment and aligning the project's goals with the overall strategic plans so the project has the greatest possible impact.

B. Assess available resources

Available resources need to be defined. What data can be reasonably gathered? How will this data be gathered? How will the information be analyzed? Will statistical software packages be required? Are funds available to cover the cost of data gathering, data analysis, software packages, consultants, data from private brokers, mass mailings, data entry, etc.? Assessment projects can be costly in terms of staff time and other resources, e.g., consultants and data analysis. However, assessments do not always need to be completed to a high level of perfection if no resources can be reasonably assigned to the effort. Sometimes, a simple effort is sufficient to achieve the project's needs.

When assessing resources, areas to consider include:

1. Are staff available to assist with the project? Availability could include staff in other parts of the organization besides the library. Staff would include personnel at all levels in the organization, since projects may need clerical, professional, and managerial staff.
2. Are there staff familiar with the area of user needs to be assessed who can assist with the project's design and completion?

3. Are there staff experienced with designing questionnaires and organizing survey projects, or would the required people be available at affordable costs? Are staff available to gather other types of data such as circulation statistics, user demographics, etc.?
4. How will the data be stored, organized, and manipulated? Does the data require the use of a relational database or statistical analysis software package, or would a spreadsheet package suffice?
5. Are there staff who can work with the software and are there staff available for data entry?
6. Are there staff available with enough experience to organize the data into a usable product?
7. Does staff or management have the analytical skills necessary to draw accurate conclusions from the data gathered?
8. Does the organization have the operational/physical plant support necessary for the project? This would include the use of computers, telephones, and printing and mail facilities.

C. Establish project scope

The scope of the project needs to be defined. Is the project's focus to investigate how to select specific materials in a single subject area, or is the intent to provide direction for resource development on a librarywide basis? The scope will indicate what types of data are needed. Develop the goals and a baseline of available resources, then basic assumptions concerning users' needs and the types of data that will be gathered may be defined. It is very important for collection/resource managers to involve library staff from many areas including reference services, circulation, and interlibrary loan to help develop basic assumptions and define the scope of the project. Staff from these areas will greatly improve the quality of the assumptions and will help provide valuable direction.

D. Define the user population

Determine whether the aim of the project is to assess needs of all potential users or a subset of the user base. Will it survey new users groups, under-served users, nonusers?

E. Review current awareness

Identify models from other organizations that have done similar studies. It does not make sense to reinvent the wheel if the work has been previously done. Remember, no two library situations are exactly the same and modifications to previous work may be necessary.

F. Identify useful information

When developing the scope of the project and defining the data to be collected, note that three basic types of information are useful:

1. Secondary or surrogate data can be used to establish the current environment.
2. Use direct information on needs to impact organizational decisions that are articulated as outcomes. Outcomes are measurable actions that affect users.
3. Data on user satisfaction should be used to test the success of the outcomes.

Projects can use all three types of data, or subsets, based on the type of project. An assessment that seeks information to aid in developing resources for new programs may only use direct user input concerning needs. A project to realign resources to the organization's strategic plan may use all three types of data. An assessment that supports a space-planning effort may use only surrogate data. It is important to understand what questions you want to ask of the data before choosing a data type and accompanying methodology.

G. Establish a time frame

Establish time lines for necessary activities. When is the completed report needed? Will the results become a necessary part of another planning cycle? Time lines are valuable in focusing the project on desired goals and help with the realistic evaluation of what can be accomplished. Certain aspects of a project will impact later stages. Establish realistic goals within the overall time frame. If the completion of the assessment has a definite deadline, it may be necessary to scale the parts of the project to fit. Some aspects may need to be discarded.

H. Complete the plan

1. Gather selected data.
2. Analyze the data for patterns or correlation with major variables. This may be difficult as many factors could impact user satisfaction with information resources. For example, collections may be adequate in size and depth to meet user needs, but bibliographic access or user education may need to be enhanced in order to see increases in use and user satisfaction data.
3. Develop outcomes. The needs assessment should lead to definite action based on data gathered. What will you do differently as a result of the assessment?
4. Assess impact of outcomes.

III. What can be measured and how to measure it: Types of assessment data that may be useful

The intent of this section is to describe briefly the types of data and data-gathering techniques that can be used to help make decisions about information resources. This is not a comprehensive discussion of sampling strategy, survey methodology, or statistical analysis techniques. This section describes basic analytical avenues most commonly found in current use. The attached bibliography contains references to several works that provide in-depth information on these topics.

A. Direct user input (e.g., user surveys)

Current quality management theories stress measuring user/customer needs. In this environment, information acquired directly from the user is given the highest consideration when developing plans for the provision of information resources. Direct user input is the most difficult data to acquire and to interpret accurately. For the purpose of these guidelines, this information falls into two general categories. The first is assessing user satisfaction with current library resources and information services. The second is assessing actual and potential use of information resources. Sometimes a survey methodology may measure both, but there is a danger in doing this if the structure and analysis of the survey instrument does not clearly distinguish between the two categories.

1. Definitions
   a) User satisfaction surveys: Satisfaction surveys are intended to gauge users' subjective impressions of library information resources and services. These surveys are used to establish relative benchmarks that can then measure change in user satisfaction over time. Only users can describe their level of satisfaction, and surveys are the most direct means to gather this information.
   b) User information use (needs) surveys: User information use or needs surveys directly measure patrons' information use patterns, users' knowledge of information resources, and their knowledge of the organization of information resources. Survey instruments must be carefully constructed to measure what patrons actually use, not what people think they use. The most effective surveys are those that solicit information that ascertains user needs rather than wants or desires.

2. Pros and cons of direct user input for needs assessment
   a) Pros:
      (1) Information coming directly from users can best describe their information needs.
      (2) Direct data has a high rate of statistical correlation. User surveys provide a high probability that the responses and data gathered really do describe users' reactions to the variables (questions) being measured. If users respond that they are happy with a service or information resource, there is a high probability that the users really are happy with that service.
      (3) When developing direct surveys, it is possible to customize the variables and ask the right questions.
      (4) It is possible to combine a library marketing or information/public relations program into the survey process.
      (5) Data gathered directly from users is often more politically powerful than static surrogate data. The information is much more persuasive to administrators when coming directly from the users. It is more robust to be

able to say: the townspeople have indicated in this survey that they want this product, or the faculty, when asked, have stated this resource is a priority.

b) Cons:

(1) The process of gathering direct user input requires significantly more resources and expertise to accomplish correctly, especially if done to valid statistical standards.

(2) Direct user survey projects require longer time frames to accomplish.

(3) "Surveyitis" may result if users feel the surveys are too frequent or intrusive. This reduces participation and the quality of results.

3. Methodology for direct user input

Two basic techniques are employed to gather information directly from users. The types vary significantly in approach and statistical validity of outcomes. Do the first technique, exploratory data gathering, to develop and test initial assumptions and to identify new and/or emerging issues. Use the second, representative/random surveys, to develop statistically valid data concerning a given population.

a) Exploratory data collection

Exploratory data collection explicitly tests library project design assumptions and reveals user perceptions concerning issues to be examined. Exploratory data collection is essentially a development process that sets the parameters for the assessment project. The goal is to discover crucial issues for the user and to discover, through exploratory (not closed ended) questioning techniques, those issues that require in depth analysis that is representative of the entire user population in question.

(1) *Focus groups.* These are "carefully planned small-group discussions designed to obtain perceptions on a defined area of interest in a permissive, nonthreatening atmosphere" (Kreuger). The power of focus groups lies in the fact that they are nondirective. Information can surface that otherwise might not emerge in a structured interview. The synergy of multiple participants creates an environment conducive to exploring new ideas. The best group size is seven to ten people who have a broad background

in the theme to be investigated. Unless the population to be sampled is very small, it is best to plan on multiple focus groups addressing the same topic in order to detect trends and patterns across groups (Kreuger 1994, 17). Developing a set of questions (no more than three or four for an hour-and-a-half meeting to allow time for each participant's input) before the group meets is important. The questions should be designed to elicit a broad range of input. One option to the one-time approach for focus groups (usually as part of a process aimed at designing a survey) would be to establish a continuing user focus group that can provide ongoing information and react to changes in information services and emerging issues over a longer period of time. Crucial components of a successful focus group include:

(a) An experienced external facilitator to moderate the meetings.

(b) Tape recorders or video cameras to record all of each focus group's activities. Bring extra tapes and backups for the recording devices. Always ask participants if they will allow the recording of the meeting before the process begins.

(c) A relaxed atmosphere with refreshments, comfortable furniture, and soft lighting.

(d) Awareness that focus-group data is highly biased and is not statistically representative of the larger client population and should not be used for broad-based decision making.

(e) Realization that the real value of focus-group information is to clarify assumptions underlying the assessment project and to assist in the development of survey instrument questions that cover the identified issues for a broad user population.

(2) *Qualitative input from surveys.* Although there are techniques to quantify qualitative information, in general the best approach is to use open-ended questions to investigate potential facets of an issue that may not be initially recognized by the library staff pursuing the assessment. These new findings may then be addressed in a system-

atic, statistically valid survey instrument to see if the new findings represent issues for the broader user group.

(3) *Crucial incident surveys.* These surveys are structured, one-on-one interviews that ask users to identify factors they consider to be crucial to their success or lack of success in obtaining desired information. Until recently, these surveys have only been used to measure user satisfaction with library public services, not to measure satisfaction with library information resources. The interview is detailed, but since the population studied is normally highly selective, the results are not statistically valid for the general user population. Yet this survey technique is valuable in identifying issues that are important to users. See the bibliography for articles that describe this technique in greater detail.

(4) *Internal staff feedback.* Collecting information from staff on their perceptions of issues affecting users can also serve to reveal issues that may be productive topics for user focus groups or surveys. Staff frequently observe user behavior, and this behavior may need to be clarified in focus groups or surveys. For example, lines to use public workstations may or may not be acceptable to users. Staff observe this behavior and can appropriately raise it as an issue, but only direct user input can define waiting in lines as a problem.

(5) *User interviews.* Frequently, the simplest and most effective way to develop information is to identify major stakeholders and just ask them how they use information, what information resources they believe they need, or similar questions. These interviews are less formal than standardized surveys designed using the principle of randomness. Major stakeholders would be those users who have a vested interest in the availability of resources: faculty at an academic/school library, physicians at a medical library, company staff at a corporate library, etc. If the population of major stakeholders is very large, interview a randomly selected sample. If the population is very small, interview all identified stakeholders. Size will be relative based upon available resources. If several staff

members are available to conduct the user interviews, then a population of 100 would not be too difficult to sample. If there is only a single staff member, it would be very difficult to perform 100 interviews. Not all approaches to user assessment will require rigorously designed processes, but most will entail, at minimum, directly asking questions of users. As this type of user interview is not as rigorous in design and execution as statistically valid direct user surveys, it can be carried out quickly and is effective in discovering issues and assumptions. Since this survey type lacks true randomness, the informal user survey will not provide statistically valid results. It is important to develop the survey questions carefully to make sure that results are useful.

b) Representative data gathering

This approach uses methods to extract information from a representative user population being considered by the project. The key criterion is statistical validity. This entails confidence in the probability that, if the survey were repeated, results would be similar given the same population demographics. The principle of randomness is crucial. All parts of the user population being surveyed should have equal chances of being selected to participate in the project.

The first step is to develop a survey instrument. Content is based on previous exploratory data gathering and on staff knowledge of issues being surveyed.

Questions to ask when approaching the design should include:

(1) *Level of specificity.* For example, is the goal of the project to develop specific information about a particular product being considered for purchase, or is the goal to develop baseline information on how users look for information, regardless of source?

(2) *Logistical load.* What resources are available for printing and processing? Keep in mind that the addition of one question also implies additional analytical work after the survey. Make sure that the length is manageable from the user's viewpoint. It is much more difficult to get consistent results from long, complex surveys because the user's

mind set changes with extended interaction with the instrument. A long survey may also restrict participation and thus confidence in the representative nature of the results.

(3) *Cross-correlation of results.* Is the survey intended to reveal patterns that can be correlated against each other? If so, comparability is dependent upon a consistent measurement technique. For example, the survey should not be designed using a multiple-choice format for one variable and open-ended questions for another variable if the two are to be compared. Also, when users are asked to rank versus rate a particular variable or set of variables, be sure to ask consistent, comparable questions.

(4) *Clarity.* Does the question really ask the intended question? A good practice is to pretest the survey with actual users to be sure that their comprehension of the questions meets your expectations.

(5) *Response rates.* To ensure a good return rate for surveys, recency and frequency data from circulation systems can be used to target survey populations. Some marketing research indicates that patrons who either use the library frequently or have used it most recently are the best respondents to surveys about the services.

c) Techniques for random surveys

Many techniques can be used to develop statistically valid random surveys. The techniques below have been widely used and discussed in the literature.

(1) Direct mailing

    (a) Pros

        i.) It is relatively easy to define and access a target population. Mailing lists of users are kept by many organizations.

        ii.) It is relatively simple to ensure the overall randomness of the survey.

        iii.) Surveys can be designed so users can respond without much difficulty. Users can mark printed forms, which can be returned in pre-addressed postage-paid envelopes. Direct mailings do not make the mistake of assuming access to electronic communication.

    (b) Cons

        i.) Direct mailing can be expensive. Return rates are often low. Follow-up mailings can increase return rates, but are costly. Postage may be an issue, as is printing. Machine scoreable forms are expensive but significantly easier to analyze with large samples.

        ii.) Sometimes the survey must be repeated until a statistically valid level of response is reached.

        iii.) These types of surveys do not allow for clarification if the responder does not understand the question.

        iv.) Computer scoreable forms do not allow for any free-form feedback from users.

    (c) Steps

        i.) Define user population(s) to be surveyed.

        ii.) Develop a statistically valid sample of the populations to be measured. A randomly generated subset of the total population is usually considered the best way to ensure a representative result. Methods of selecting random samples can be found in all general statistical texts, with random number tables as addenda. Random lists can be generated by many database management, statistical, or spreadsheet software packages. For a more detailed explanation of the reasons and methods of random sampling, see Arthur W. Hafner's *Descriptive Statistical Techniques for Librarians*, published in 1997 by the American Library Association, or Floyd J. Fowler's *Survey Research Methods*, published in 1993 by Sage Publications.

        iii.) The sample needs to be sufficiently large so a statistically valid population can be acquired even though the total proportion of returns is small. A backup group can be developed using the same criteria that can be used if the first sampling effort fails for some reason (flawed survey, etc.).

iv.) Follow-up is important to achieving a usable sample response. A simple technique to improve the response rate is to call potential survey respondents to make sure they received the survey and to take the opportunity to stress the importance of participating in the survey. Note that overzealous follow-up can have a negative impact if respondents feel that the contact is an invasion of privacy.

v.) Return instructions should be clear. Make the form as easy as possible to fill out and include a stamped, return-addressed envelope. Incentives (such as a dollar bill) often help get attention, especially if the population is heavily surveyed from other sources.

vi.) Establish deadlines for response and decide in advance if a second, follow-up mailing will go out. Follow-up mailings often ensure an adequate response to mail surveys.

Direct mailings measure user response, but the overall quality can be suspect since there is no immediate opportunity to interact with the users to discover their perceived needs. Survey design is crucial, but there are tradeoffs in terms of the range of responses from the user.

(2) Online forms

Online forms are digital surveys that are administered over electronic mail (e-mail), an internal network such as an intranet, or external Internet or graphical Web environment. These surveys are either available on an ongoing basis or broadcast at chosen intervals.

The growing appeal of using the Web or the Internet for surveys is due to the more manageable logistics. Printing and postage costs are avoided: The results are already in digital format so it is much easier to transfer the data to a spreadsheet or statistical package for analysis and report generation. It is also fairly simple to deliver the survey to the target population and for them to respond. Because these surveys can be tied to real-time use of a service (appended to an online index, for instance), there is the advantage of getting the response when the experience is freshest.

Ensuring the validity of the population sample is a concern with the online survey method. Not all possible library users are regular users of e-mail and other online resources. If the online form is an ongoing user response form attached to a local automated system or in a single Web site, it might be susceptible to ballot stuffing. Since the form is open to anyone using the system (password protected or not), maintaining a heterogeneous demographic response is difficult. Online surveys work best when a survey form is targeted randomly to an e-mail list that is drawn across the population. Ongoing user response forms are best used to gauge user satisfaction longitudinally. It is important to remember that the online environment automatically limits the user population and therefore can introduce a biased sample.

A basic tenet of survey strategy is guaranteeing anonymity to respondents. This is difficult to guarantee in the electronic environment. One option would be to supply a mailing address to which users could send a completed paper copy of the survey.

A good example of using online surveys in a Web environment is provided by the Georgia Institute of Technology's Graphic, Visualization, & Usability Center's ongoing survey of Web users, www.cc.gatech.edu/gvu/user_surveys/. This survey has been conducted several times since 1994. The results of the various surveys are available at the Web site.

(a) Pros of online surveys

    i.) Online surveys are logistically cheaper to administer (no postage, paper, etc).

    ii.) The surveys can be organized to produce longitudinal studies.

    iii.) Online surveys are effective for measuring user satisfaction at the time an information product or service is used.

    iv.) The surveys can be analyzed faster than paper forms because the responses are already in digital format.

(b) Cons of online surveys

    i.) The use of the surveys assumes broad user facility with electronic systems, e-mail, or use of the Internet.

    ii.) Ensuring the security or confidentiality of the responses can be difficult.

    iii.) Controlling the target population and ensuring the randomness of the responses is difficult.

    iv.) Eliciting responses from users is difficult. They can easily ignore surveys.

    v.) The electronic system serving as the platform may crash or have other difficulties, and the survey receives negative reactions based on system performance.

(3) Randomly timed surveys

These surveys are conducted at the point of service or at the time a collection is used. The timing of the survey is selected randomly to ensure that all activity will have an equal chance of being surveyed. An example is a direct user interview conducted immediately upon completion of a service transaction, or a user survey that occurs in a specific area of a collection, separate collection, or branch library at the actual time a patron is using that collection. This type of survey is conducted at random intervals over a period of time in order to provide a statistically valid sample of the identified user population.

(a) Conducting a randomly timed survey

    i.) Determine the overall time line for project.

    ii.) Determine the total possible hours available for contacting users and assign numbers to blocks of time.

    iii.) Use these numbers as the universe that the random sample will be drawn from and, using a random number generator and random time table or similar device, develop a list of random time blocks to be surveyed.

    iv.) During these periods of time, either distribute the survey to users in the chosen area or conduct one-on-one interviews.

(b) Pros

    i.) Users respond to randomly timed surveys when their perceptions of their use of the information resource or service are freshest.

    ii.) Direct interviews allow for immediate follow-up questions and the clarification of misunderstood questions. This quality would apply to all direct interviews, not just those associated with randomly timed surveys.

    iii.) Random surveys are an effective means to gauge a collection's use over a long period of time.

(c) Cons

    i.) Randomly timed surveys require significant resources and planning. Staff are needed to distribute forms or conduct interviews at timed intervals.

    ii.) Users may have negative reactions to the survey, feeling it interrupts their library activity.

    iii.) It is difficult to ensure a heterogeneous sample of the entire user population. After conducting the survey, it is necessary to look for patterns of responses that may indicate that despite a random selection of times for the survey, unforeseen variables have provided inconsistent results.

B. Secondary information:
Data that describes current conditions

Secondary, or surrogate, information is indirectly representative of user information resource use patterns. While typically easier to obtain, it is more difficult to use secondary information effectively. There is no direct correlation between surrogate data and the actual use of or need for information by library patrons, but the data is often useful in providing information for decision making processes. Secondary data can describe the current environment at a macro level when used in conjunction with a broader spectrum of data. An example would be the use of academic departments' student enrollment figures, or simple demographic studies to reallocate library budgetary resources. In a university setting, one could look at enrollment figures by department. For instance, if the Economics Department has 15 percent of the enrollment, 15 percent of the materials budget could be allocated to support the department. For a public library, if 20 percent of the local population is under the age of twelve, 20 percent of the budget could be allocated to purchasing children's materials. The underlying assumption that there should be a direct correlation between enrollment/population share and resource allocation can often be misleading. This approach ignores significant variables, such as actual use patterns and the relative availability and cost of materials in that subject/service area. Surrogate data may describe the macro environment but does not describe actual needs or library patrons' use of resources. It is very useful in defining the current environment and the demographic characteristics of the user base. Although secondary information does not directly describe user information needs, a planning process for information services that includes good secondary data is useful.

We generally choose secondary data for assessments because it is relatively easy to obtain and requires no surveying or statistical analysis to incorporate into planning processes. As organizations have increased their levels of automation, there is greater access to more types of data, especially circulation statistics, student enrollment, and user demographic profiles. These types of data can be used to define the current environment and to develop user population profiles to target subsequent direct sampling of users. Secondary data is easiest to use when it can be manipulated in a spreadsheet or database manager. However, it may be that the data exists only on paper. This data would then need to be input to a spreadsheet or other system for analysis.

The following procedures represent some basic steps for developing secondary data. These steps can be repeated for most of the data types discussed in this section:

1. Determine the format and file structure required for the data. Will a relational database, spreadsheet, or statistical software package be used to store and organize the data? Will structure for the data be established through organizing it by user group, academic department, subject, service point, etc.?

2. If working with an outside group to obtain data, contact sources for the data and determine availability. Clearly communicate your needs, format requirements, and intentions for the use of the data.
3. Review received data for completeness and accuracy.
4. Determine overall data structure for the project. What are the organizing points and the linking points in the database or spreadsheet? Will the data be organized by academic unit and subject, with links between subject and unit? Another example: Will the data be organized by user group and service point, with links between the two?
5. Transfer the data into whatever system is going to be used to store and organize the project.
6. Check transfer for accuracy.

Pros:

1. Secondary data is relatively inexpensive to obtain.
2. Statistical information that is consistently gathered over a period of time makes it easier to do longitudinal studies of change. The information is also useful for comparing peer institutions to one another. Examples of these types of established data include U.S. census data, ARL statistics, or annual book trade and publishing figures.
3. Secondary data is easy to manipulate and to incorporate into planning documents and reports.
4. Secondary data can be developed and used in relatively short periods of time.
5. Secondary data requires little in the way of special training, software, or survey/interview expertise.

Cons:

1. Secondary data is not articulated with outcomes. It does not reveal what the users are really doing to obtain information nor how external factors, such as the addition of effective document delivery, affect changes in user information-seeking behavior.
2. Secondary data is sometimes used assuming that it reflects current users' behaviors. But due to the data's historical na-

ture, the information may represent conditions that are not
valid to today's users.

3. Decisions based on secondary data should be followed up with
longitudinal user satisfaction surveys to determine cause/
effect of changes in resource allocations, services, or user demographics.

4. It is difficult to develop correlations between various types of
secondary data. For example, how does the in-house use of
journals correlate with the number of students or other user
populations?

C. Specific types of secondary data

1. Demographic data

This is the quantitative description of the primary or secondary
groups that use the library. Academic libraries focus on faculty
and student populations; K–12 libraries focus on the faculty, parent groups, and student populations; corporate libraries examine
the clientele identified by the parent organization; and public libraries focus on the community they serve.

There are several sources for demographic data. Local circulation systems can contain information on local user populations.
For academic and K–12 libraries, administrative offices will
maintain data on faculty populations and student enrollments.
For public libraries, demographic information may be available
from city, county, or state planning offices or from state or fed-
eral government agencies. Census figures are the basis of most
demographic analyses. Certain private companies can provide
(for a fee) customized demographic analyses. Demographic variables include age, ethnicity, household income, educational level,
and other data that have surrogate meaning for projecting library
demand levels. Corporate libraries consult with human resource
divisions to identify customer groups.

a) Specific demographic data for academic libraries

(1) *Number of graduate students or undergraduate students*: These numbers are generally available in more
than one counting unit, typically available either as
head count or full-time equivalency (FTE). Head count,
the total number of individuals enrolled at a specific
time, and FTE, the total number of individuals divided

by local definition of full-time credit hour load, are very different numbers. It is advisable to know your information needs before approaching central administration for the data.

(2) *Degrees awarded*: This is the actual number of degrees awarded, organized by academic department and type of degree.

(3) *Faculty/staff demographics*: This information can be obtained from data maintained at many institutions' personnel, planning, or other administrative units. Variables that might be valuable in a surrogate analysis are rank and unit or department affiliation. There are two basic sources for this data. The personnel and/or payroll office of the parent organization will maintain data files on employees. This would be true for academic and corporate libraries. Also, some information will be maintained in local circulation systems.

b) Specific demographic data for public libraries

Census figures are the basis of most demographic analyses done in textual or Geographic Information System (GIS) format. Demographic variables include age, ethnicity, household income, educational level, and other data sets that have surrogate meaning for projecting library demand levels. Data such as group incomes, sales distributions, unemployment rates, types of occupations, and distribution of work activities may also be available. This information may be maintained by city, county, or state planning offices, or it may be necessary to gather this data from published business sources. In some situations the data may not be available and needs to be developed through surveys or other means. Sometimes it is useful to compare data from circulation systems with user demographic information as this will indicate which user populations are using the library.

2. Number and distribution of student enrollment credit hours

These statistics are generally derived from a school's enrollment database. Not all internal information systems can supply these numbers. The number and distribution of student enrollment credit hours is a better indicator of potential user needs than simple head counts, or FTEs. Credit hour data reflects what courses are really being taken by students. This data is best looked at over a period of years since all courses are not offered each semester.

3. Course offerings
   In addition to looking at current credit hour enrollment, it is important to assess course offerings longitudinally over at least two years. Some courses are not offered every semester or academic year and may not be reflected in credit hour enrollments. It is now common for colleges and universities to use Web sites to distribute course catalogs. Downloading the data from a Web site to a usable format for manipulation in a software application may be problematic. Current changes in faculty, administration, and new directions for curriculum may not be reflected in course catalogs, but will have an impact on course offerings and should be reviewed as part of the process of looking at course offerings.

4. Electronic resources use statistics
   Electronic information resources are the fastest growing part of libraries' information services. It is increasingly important that the use of these products is documented and understood so fiscal resources can be used effectively to provide the best electronic access. Organizations cannot afford to provide expensive electronic access tools that patrons do not use. One barrier to gathering data on patrons' use is the multiple platforms that libraries use to provide access to electronic information. In some situations a single public workstation can access data from the local OPAC, CD-ROM networks, local wide area servers, the Internet, and the World Wide Web. It is difficult to measure actual use of specific products when several system interfaces are used. The constant change that occurs as files are moved from platform to platform compounds this problem. Data that helps describe the use of electronic information is crucial as resources are being heavily invested in these services and hard decisions are being made concerning the internal allocation of resources to provide electronic information. There are no easy, comprehensive solutions for developing valid statistics on patron use of electronic resources by directly asking users what they use, how they use the product, and how successful their efforts were.

However, there are means available to develop data concerning the use of electronic information.

Detailed information describing patron use of Web and Internet information sources is hard to gather automatically in local systems. At this time, the most important sources for this information are the publishers of the electronic products. In many situations, the electronic publishers (EPs) can provide data concerning the local use of their products. This data may include the number of searches that have been performed, the number of log-ons, the length of the sessions, the number of records used, the specific parts of the database accessed, and possibly a summary of the actual searches. This type of data gathering is not available equally from all EPs. The capability to gather data that describes local use of Web/Internet products needs to be clarified at the time of purchase. If possible, write the specifications for the collection and distribution of local use data into the product license.

A growing number of log analysis tools are available for use in capturing information about the use of Web resources. There are several references to these software packages in the bibliography and the list of Web resources. These analysis tools provide Web authors with information on the use of their sites. However, these programs could be used to track local activity and provide some data on patrons' use of electronic information. This is a new, emerging area in software development. More powerful tools should be available in the near future.

The use of Web "counters" has become popular. Most Web pages have a mechanism that counts the number of times users access a Web page. Such counters provide basic information on how often a page is accessed. These counts don't describe the real use of the information, only the fact that someone visited the page. Also, due to the way information is stored and distributed in the Web, counters cannot accurately measure the real use of a site since multiple uses of the page in the same user session will go uncounted.

Some local OPACs provide information concerning how often gateways to external data are used. This capability varies from system to system. A library's systems office can determine if the local integrated library system (ILS) contains specific data and how to access the data. Again, these may be basic counts of a gateway's usage and may not describe how the information was used.

Some types of electronic resources, such as locally mounted journal indexes and other databases on local CD-ROM or hard drives, provide access to use statistics through the library's OPAC or access to use data through the user interface that provides access to the CD-ROM or other locally mounted data. This capability varies from system to system. It is important to consult with the systems offices to determine if this information is available from local resources. In addition, stand-alone metering softwares can be purchased and used to measure how often individual databases are used. Frequently, the same metering systems can also profile the actual search strategies and the success/failure of the strategies. This data might include subjects searched, number of searches, number of hits, number of citations downloaded, printing activity, etc. Although this information can sometimes be generated automatically by some data systems' software, in other situations the addition of metering software may be necessary to track usage of local systems in a quality way. As with all monitoring of user activity, it is important to maintain individual user confidentiality. This includes use of the Internet, the Web, and other online activities.

System-produced data may not provide all the information necessary to evaluate use of electronic resources. It may be necessary to develop other techniques to gather information on how users are really interacting with electronic products. These techniques could include random, timed, direct user surveys, or electronic survey forms that poll users at the time they are using the system.

5. Circulation statistics
   Circulation statistics provide some of the most valuable secondary information. Circulation statistics describe a major subset of the resources that are being used. There may not be a direct correlation between current use and future needs, but the data gives valuable insight into the current use patterns. It is crucial to keep in mind that circulation figures record only the actual use of items when circulated. These figures do not quantify patrons' use of materials within the library or their use of noncirculating

collections. When this data is combined with user surveys, the resulting information gives the best quantitative description of user information-seeking behaviors. The data can be used to assess the cost-effectiveness of many library information services, including the analysis of the cost-effectiveness of serial collections (how many uses compared to subscription costs) as well as the performance of approval plans (how many titles circulated within a defined period of time).

Local online systems generally provide circulation statistics. Organization of the data is crucial so the data can be sorted or compiled into categories that can be linked directly to user groups, subject areas, or areas of librarian's bibliographic responsibility. This is frequently more feasible for academic libraries since user groups can be linked to academic departments, which can be linked to broad subject areas. For example, it can be assumed that the students in the English as a Second Language program are affiliated with the English faculty, who use the LC class P materials. Public libraries will have more difficulty linking broad user populations with specific subject collections. For basic steps in gathering and working with this data, see III B, paragraph 3: Basic steps.

In libraries without online circulation systems, if it is absolutely necessary to develop circulation statistics, then random timed surveys might be used to develop data that describes circulation activity.

There are a number of basic strategies that can be used to gather circulation/use statistics. The following are the most common.

a) *Circulation patterns of monographic/serial collections.* These statistics involve the actual count of monographs, journals, and other materials that are checked out from a particular library or service point. Numbers can be organized by subject, patron status, library location, or academic unit, depending on the needs of the analysis and the ability of the local circulation system to produce the data. Circulation data is a strong indicator of what materials are being used by patrons; however, it does not document in-house use, journal use (for noncirculating collections), or use of electronic titles. Historical collecting patterns and current purchasing patterns impact patron use since available materials circulate. It is valuable to develop circulation data as a percentage of collection size to provide good comparative information. For example, 300 titles in a 3,000-title literature collection circulated in the last year (10 percent), while 50 titles in a 100-title computer self-help collection circulated in the last year (50 percent). If one looked simply at the raw numbers, one could assume that literature is the most heavily used collection. If circulation as a percentage of collection size is analyzed, another conclusion can be reached.

b) *Statistics derived from patron requests for holds/recalls on currently circulating materials.* This set of statistics counts the actual number of requests for titles that are currently checked out. This is a measure of demand for individual items and overall patterns of unmet need.

c) *In-house use statistics for both serials and monographs.* These statistics measure the use of materials used within the library. Most often, in-house use statistics are gathered by counting items as they are picked up and reshelved. Computer scanning devices that read information from bar codes on each item can be used to gather data on reshelving activity. More often, in-house use data is still gathered by hand. Randomly timed surveys are economical approaches to developing in-house use data without having to create a system that counts every item that is picked up for reshelving every day.

d) *Photocopy activity.* This is the measurement of patron in-house use of photocopy services to copy library materials. Photocopy statistics are commonly developed by extracting information from patron request forms submitted to the library's photocopy service, gathered from the reshelving process of materials left at photocopy machines, or developed from randomly timed surveys of patrons as they make use of photocopy services. Integrated library systems do not keep this data. In addition, photocopy machines can track the number of pages copied, and cost receipts are also available. These types of data will indicate overall use of the photocopy service, but cannot indicate use by subject or by patron type.

e) *Gate counts of the number of users entering a library building.* Many libraries have installed security systems that, in addition to protecting collections from theft, can count the number of times an area has been entered. Most automatic systems keep a simple head count. Some systems require a user card to gain admittance. Card-based systems can provide more specific data, such as patron type. Gate counts indicate overall traffic in a specific physical location, but do not necessarily measure the use of the collections or services.

f) *Use of media.* Data that could be reviewed includes in-house use of materials and equipment; rental of films, videos, or other media; circulation of films from local collections; the scheduling of media equipment; and room scheduling. This data documents user demand for these materials.

6. Collection statistics and evaluation of collections
   Whenever an assessment of user information needs is attempted, it is useful to have a profile of the local library's collections and other information resources as a baseline for analysis. There are many different approaches to working with collection statistics, the most detailed being the conspectus methodologies developed by the Research Library Group (RLG) and the Western Library Network (WLN).

   The conspectus approach uses a detailed, hierarchical subject structure (based on the Library of Congress or Dewey classification schedules) as a framework for a quantitative and qualitative assessment of an institution's collections. It also establishes detailed criteria that can be applied during the assessment, so each institution is using the same system to develop internal measures. The conspectus methodology provides a common language to communicate the relative strengths and weaknesses of library collections. This is particularly important in developing baseline information for consortial sharing and collection building projects.

   There are many different ways to measure collections. Statistics concerning collection size and subject distribution can be drawn from local automated systems. Manual counts may need to be done if collection statistics are not available from online systems. A simple methodology that can be used to manually develop collection statistics is to randomly draw a sample from a shelflist and determine how many cards are in each centimeter and then measure the entire shelflist. This measurement can be organized by subject class. This methodology has been used successfully by the American Library Association (ALA) Association for Library Collections & Technical Services (ALCTS) *North American Title Count.* Another resource that details approaches to collection evaluation is the *Guide to the Evaluation of Library Collections* published by the Collection Management & Development Committee, Resources Section, Resources and Technical Services Division, the predecessor of ALCTS, American Library Association. The guide describes in practical terms several methods for evaluating library collections.

Collection statistics can also be derived from a library's digital bibliographic archives held by national utilities (OCLC, RLIN, etc.). A library can negotiate with its utility to produce a tape of bibliographic data that could then be loaded into a local database management system for analysis. A library might also be able to contract with a utility to produce the analysis. These approaches can be expensive, as the utilities will charge for developing the data and for the manipulation and analysis of the data.

Another source of collection statistics, OCLC's CD-ROM product, the Collection Analysis CD, uses the last ten years of a library's monographic OCLC records and creates a statistical analysis of the library's holdings compared to selected peer libraries' holdings. However, the 1998 edition of this tool will be the last published by OCLC. All of these methods will only quantify those titles that were cataloged using the specific bibliographic utility.

For all of these approaches, plans for the use of the collection information must be determined before the data is gathered so that the results can be organized to correlate with user information. For academic libraries this might entail the development of links between subject classifications and academic departments. For public libraries this might entail the development of links between collections and demographically distinct user groups.

Types of information that can be gathered from collection studies include:

a) *Number of titles/volumes*: This information is normally available from local automated systems and is usually organized by subject, material type, or location. If the data is not available online, manual counts can be conducted using averaging techniques. This involves developing a random sample of what will be measured, whether it is number of shelves or the size of the shelflist. Counts of this sort require significant resources to complete. Quantitative measures of collections represent historical patterns of resource allocation; the measures do not represent current collecting emphasis or patron needs, nor are the measures indicative of future needs.

b) *Median age of collections*: These statistics describe the relative age of a collection based on the publication date; the median age being the point at which half the collection was published after the date and half the collection published prior to the date. The library catalog usually provides this information. If the catalog cannot provide the information, then a sampling/averaging manual technique would need to be employed. Publication age can reveal gaps and trends in collections and provide information that can help develop preservation plans. The age of the collection does not provide direct data to describe user needs or user population groups but can be useful when analyzing circulation data for specific user groups—i.e., if the section on computer books has a median age of ten years, this can contribute to low circulation.

c) *Condition of collection*: This data describes the relative repair and replacement levels broken out by subject areas of the collection. The physical condition of the collection can be a surrogate indicator of use and can be tracked longitudinally. Often the physical condition can best be determined as part of a preservation study. Assessments of physical condition and age of a collection provide two basic types of information:

   (1) Surrogate data concerning use patterns. Worn bindings are an indicator of use just as dust and lack of wear indicate lack of use. It is important to note that this data does not necessarily have a direct correlation to current or developing user needs. Tracking the patterns of use (both in-house and circulating) and correlating these patterns with publishing dates and the age of materials will provide a better profile of the possibility of continued use of specific collections or segments of collections. Much of the data concerning use is anecdotal. Wear can take many forms and can result from many sources. The book may have been purchased used, and the title has never been

used by local users. Indicators of lack of use are also anecdotal. The amount of dust is relative and again can be
altered by several factors besides use or lack of use. This
type of data can be problematic, yet can provide insight
into use/nonuse of collections.

(2) Preservation studies can identify collections that may not
be able to support continued usage in their present state.
There is a tension between the needs for preserving collections and current user needs. Some materials may need
to be preserved or new copies of high-use items acquired.
When developing resource plans, it is important not to include collections that require significant conservation as
active resources to be used by users without planning for
preservation.

d) *Distribution of multiple copies in the collection*: Analyze the
use of multiple copies in the library by studying circulation
statistics. Online systems normally provide this data, although
some systems may require a separate statistical analysis software package to develop the data. User demand can be indicated by the existence of multiple copies and their location.
Care should be taken, however, to identify copies that represent actual use patterns by correlating the information with
circulation statistics.

7. Interlibrary loan (ILL) and document delivery statistics
This data describes the number and subject of interlibrary loan
and document delivery requests processed for library users. It
serves as a record of local use of materials that the library has obtained from other sources. The use of local systems to process
and track ILL requests is relatively new. Consequently, local online systems are not good sources for data concerning ILL activity over many years. The OCLC and RLIN networks are the current primary sources for ILL data because at this time these
networks are the primary conduits for ILL activity. If a commercial document delivery service is used to supply all or a portion
of users' requests, data may be available from the supplier. Certain software programs can compile ILL data from OCLC
records, or other spreadsheet or database management software
may need to be used to manipulate the data from these systems
and create a reasonable set of reports that describe ILL activity.

The ILL portion of several online systems is being developed and the above scenario is changing. Currently, however, the data from national utilities, compiled by secondary software, is the best means for developing interlibrary loan reports. These reports can be organized by subject, patron type, material type, date/time of use, academic affiliation, etc. ILL data is a relative indicator of demand for information that is not being met by locally available resources. The data can be hard to interpret since a lack of borrowing requests could indicate decline in user interest due to poor service or lack of user awareness of the service, or it could indicate that local collections meet user needs. Increases in ILL could indicate growing problems in collection strength in terms of meeting patrons' needs, or could indicate problems educating users to find materials or problems with bibliographic access. Despite problems with interpretation, ILL data has several uses:

a) ILL data can be compared to budget allocations and/or collection policies to determine if the resources provided are aligned with allocations and collection goals. In other words, the highest ILL activities should not appear in areas where resources have been concentrated.

b) ILL statistics can also be indicative of emerging or shifting user interests.

c) ILL statistics can point to resource weakness if significant activity occurs in unexpected areas.

d) ILL statistics can also be a measure of the effectiveness of cooperative resource-sharing agreements.

When setting up the software that compiles ILL statistics, it is advisable to assess the potential use for the information. Data concerning borrower type or subject matter requested can greatly enhance the value of ILL data. User confidentiality needs to be a consideration when working with ILL data.

8. Consortial agreements
   Consortial arrangements that have a mission to share information resources among a group of libraries are becoming more common. If the parent organization is a member of broader consortia, then the agreements that define the relationship need to be reviewed during assessment projects. Resource strengths and weaknesses as well as the intensity of resource development should be addressed in the agreement. The agreement itself

might be a good source of data concerning collections and their use. Some agreements may also contain data concerning consortial partners. This group would have an impact on use statistics. The patrons from consortial partners need to be considered as part of the local library's user base; when data is analyzed, the impact of this group needs to be considered. Information from consortial agreements can reveal possible factors impacting circulation, interlibrary loan and document delivery data, and external use of electronic resources. High ILL transactions in a given subject area may reflect a consortial agreement rather than an unintentional weakness in the collection. For example, high ILL use of the history collection may not indicate that the library's history collection does not meet local patrons' needs. It may be an indicator that the collection is heavily used by consortial partners since it was to be developed as the group's history collection. Examination of these agreements can reveal the scope of collecting or information resource use behavior and help define external users who might otherwise not be profiled in the analysis.

9. Price indexes and other cost data

    The development of local information resources does not occur in a vacuum. Pricing and availability reflect national and international market conditions and publishing trends. The changes in the average cost of books and serials, combined with changes in the number of titles published, are important points to consider. Information concerning publishing trends is available from several sources:

    a) Price indexes for books and serials published in the United States, Western Europe, and Latin America are published annually in *The Bowker Annual of Library and Book Trade Information* by the American Library Association's Library Materials Price Index Committee.

    b) Journal cost data and costs/coverage reports for monographic approval plans are available from several book and serial vendors. In some instances these reports are available on the vendor's Web home page.

    c) Most major materials vendors can supply cost reports upon request.

    d) A literature search will also reveal many sources for cost data as several journals publish articles each year on this topic.

Generally, the data is arranged by broad subject area and normally includes the number of titles, average price per title, and percentage change from the previous year. The data can be used as a document that informs allocation assumptions that can be tested against assessment results. Normally price information is in text format in the previously mentioned sources and will need to be rekeyed into a local software application for further manipulation.

The price and availability data needs to be part of any assessment that looks at allocations for the materials budget. For example, an allocation scheme that does not recognize the disparity between the costs of chemistry books and books in psychology misses a major piece of data that drives resource development in those respective areas. An assessment could identify a small number of titles in a subject area. This may not represent a potential gap in a collection as much as it reflects the absolute availability of materials published in that subject area. There may be few titles published in that particular area, and consequently there is a small collection.

The foreign exchange rate needs to be examined regularly as fluctuations can cause changes in the ability to purchase foreign materials. If a foreign currency falls sharply against the U.S. dollar, then an area supported by publications from that country may add materials more quickly than planned. If the dollar falls against a foreign currency, resource plans may fall short of goals.

10. Analysis of organizations' external environment

    Organizational planning documents define the environment in which any resource needs assessment occurs. On the other hand, assessment projects should inform organizational planning efforts. There are many different ways that organizations can develop documentation to describe the existing organizational environment. One popular approach has been to analyze and evaluate internal conditions (strengths and weaknesses) and external factors (opportunities and threats) that affect the organization. Often the library and the parent organization generate planning documents. The following types of data can be developed:

    a) Current situational analyses (CSA) are detailed descriptions of environmental factors (e.g., inflation, policy changes, new technology, etc.) that may have immediate impact on the organization. Often the CSA includes political, municipal, and/or legislative changes that will affect the library.

b) Strategic plans represent the overall goals and identified priorities of the organization. These plans sometimes contain information that can be used to assist assessment projects. For example, if the parent organization has set a goal of increased access to electronic information, this information is used to establish basic assumptions for the needs assessment. Also, these documents sometimes contain data concerning the external environment, the organization's budget situation, the regional political climate, and possibly user input from other assessments. Strategic plans should be widely available within the organization or may be obtained from administrative personnel. The reports are generally text and sometimes include extensive data attachments. It may be necessary to contact original authors to obtain base data in a usable electronic format.

Note: This section is included to indicate that when doing an assessment, it is wise to look at documents that describe the overall strategic environment of the library and the parent organization. It is not implied that these activities must be conducted as part of an assessment of users' needs. If documents exist that describe the organization's external environment, use them.

11. Materials budget as secondary data

The materials budget is the part of the overall library budget that is spent on books, serials, electronic information resources, etc. Library materials budgets often reflect librarians' perceptions of patron demands for materials. Materials budgets can also reflect, to some degree, direct patron requests. Overall, the budget should act as an indirect record of current user demand. In some cases it reflects patterns of expenditures that may have a long history. The collection development unit, an administrative unit, or the acquisitions unit can provide materials budget information. Sometimes local integrated library systems can provide more detailed reports on library expenditures than what might be available in prepared budget reports.

12. Citation analyses

Citation analyses are the critical review of bibliographic citations in order to determine levels of usage and are used almost exclusively in the academic library environment, and to a lesser degree in corporate and other special libraries. These studies reflect only reported usage (i.e., citations), not the totality of information that patrons use. Citation analyses create a profile of those journals and monographs that are cited in the literature published by faculty and other local library users. These studies can be useful in comparing the proportion of local vs. external information resources used by authors in given disciplines, and may have implications for resource allocation.

Citation analyses can be done by developing a random survey technique. Select a representative group of authors (or, in the case of one academic department, choose all faculty members) that you want to profile. Contact the authors to obtain a current list of their publications. If these are not available, then use standard bibliographic sources, including journal indexes in their field to develop a source list to check. Search their work for citations to other works and record these in an appropriate format (spreadsheet, relational database, etc.). This data indicates some level of the resources used. Citation analyses are not a direct model of user behavior as the citations do not include the full universe of information resources consulted by a given user in the research process.

Another approach for citation studies is the development of lists of journals that currently cite local authors' publications. This type of data may not be directly applicable to an assessment of user needs, but can be part of an assessment of the quality of scholarly activity in a given discipline. The Institute for Scientific Information (ISI) publishes journal citation indexes, available in print or electronic database form. These indexes are useful for analyzing the correlation between a local collection and the core literature of a specific discipline or research topic being published by local faculty. This is a useful tool for identifying those journals with articles that cite local authors. It remains necessary to select the set of authors to be studied, but using a citation index makes the process less cumbersome. Performing a simple search by author provides lists of journals citing the selected author's works. Do not confuse this analysis as a surrogate for how a local author is using a local collection. A great deal of material may be used, but not cited in the final work.

13. Journal impact rankings and useful half-life ratings
The Institute for Scientific Information produces annual analyses, based on citations reported in its indexes, in the sciences, social sciences, and humanities. The impact factor is a longitudinal algorithm that can be used to rank journals based on the number of times their articles are cited by other authors. It is a use measure. By tracking citation frequency over time, half-life analysis indicates the relative useful life span of journals in terms of volume of citation.

ISI also publishes annual lists of journals that rank these titles by how many citations the journals receive in other journals. In this way, a measure is established of the relative impact within a discipline of each journal. The more often a journal is cited in other journals, the higher the impact of that journal on its discipline.

ISI also provides a statistically driven measure of the useful life span of journals, called a half-life index, by measuring the number of article citations over a period of time. The half-life indicates relative activity levels for journals and can be useful in deciding when to archive, move to remote storage, change format (digitization, microfilm, or purchase completely in electronic format), or otherwise preserve journals.

ISI does not provide universal or exhaustive coverage for all subject areas in journals. To either supplement the ISI data or gain finer resolution at the local use level, it may be necessary to conduct analyses of works published by local authors.

14. Measure of actual use of journals
There is a significant use of materials that occurs within the physical walls of a library that is never recorded in circulation systems but is a useful surrogate for current user needs. This is especially true for in-house journal usage, particularly in libraries where current periodicals are not circulated.

In-house use of journal collections can be studied using a number of different methods. The best approach is to record all in-house reshelving activity. Procedures can be established that record all reshelving, but this requires an assignment of substantial resources to record and compile all the data. In-house journal use studies do not necessarily require rigorous data collection on a continuing basis. Journal use studies can be accomplished by statistically valid spot-checks of reshelving activity over a significant period of time. Over the course of the study period, record all journals at random intervals.

Considering the costs and the high rate of inflation, good data on how patrons use journals is very important to have. Usage statistics can be effective in communicating to users why a given journal was cancelled or retained, and for identifying use throughout the entire collection.

Use studies do have their problems since users can quite easily have a negative impact on the data. Despite frequent requests not to do so, some users will always reshelve materials. Other patrons will deliberately remove materials from the shelf to boost use numbers. It may be necessary to design a program of random user observation to determine what variables might be impacting journal use data.

15. Other library activities

    Data concerning users' information needs can be derived from other less formal means, such as activity at reference desks or other service sites. These types of data can detail what types of materials are being sought by users in these transactions. This data may not be readily available. Randomly timed surveys of staff in these areas may be an effective approach. Also, having staff record detailed transaction logs at random intervals is another effective approach.

    In addition, the composition of the noncirculating collections (usually the reference and special collections areas) can be indicators of high use of the materials in these collections, or the composition could be an indicator that these materials are highly valued. Shelving statistics can quantify use in these areas. Size and age of these collections are also baseline data for assessments. If these statistics are not available from an online system, then a manual shelflist measurement project can supply them. Use caution when interpreting any patterns drawn from data about the noncirculating collections. Composition and use patterns may correlate with programmatic changes (for example), or the use patterns may be linked to other variables. Something may have superseded the need for specific tools—a new electronic database might duplicate a printed title, for example—and therefore impact the measurement of use. Another variable that might affect the use of the reference collection is the intensity or effectiveness of user instruction and how well reference staff interact with key patron groups. In addition, the currency, quality, and location of the collection vis-à-vis the user pool will impact use.

IV. Scenarios for user needs assessments

The following section provides a few samples of the process for conducting user needs assessments and the types of data to use during specific types of needs assessment projects. We do not intend for the scenarios to be all inclusive, nor should you use the scenarios as precise blueprints for assessments. The scenarios provide a look at how the various approaches may be combined logically in a single project.

A. New degree program

A college or university has determined that a new major or degree program will be offered. The library wants to develop a plan to provide information resources to support the program.

1. Develop assumptions concerning the goals of the assessment project and develop ideas concerning what the faculty and students in the program will need. Set a time line.
2. Consult institutional strategic plans and other reports concerning the establishment of the new program. Define the project's scope.
3. Identify resources that can be used for the assessment.
4. Develop baseline data concerning faculty, staff, and students who the program would support. This data would include number of enrolled students, degrees offered, active faculty, courses offered, affiliated research, or interdisciplinary programs.
5. Conduct a citation analysis of the faculty in the new program. This provides an overall picture of how the library needs to support the program and can indicate specific new resources to supply.
6. Hold focus groups with selected faculty and prospective students.

7. Interview several program principals in depth to follow up on themes revealed in focus groups and to gather other pertinent information on goals of the new program.
8. Analyze data from interviews and focus groups. Compare information on stated needs with initial library staff assumptions. Prepare summary report to library and users.
9. Conduct a baseline study of currently available local resources. This would include collection statistics on print and journal holdings, access to electronic information, and access to document delivery services. Currently available local resources could also include materials in other disciplines that might be used to support the new program, e.g., statistics in the social sciences, or interdisciplinary links such as area studies.
10. Develop a plan for meeting the needs of the program.

B. Possible scenario regarding the reallocation of materials budget

The library may find itself in the position where there have not been major changes in the overall allocation process for some time. Over the years, serials inflation and the need to provide access to electronic resources have seriously eroded spending in some areas. New customer groups that did not exist in the past now require support. The library needs to reassess the way it spends its materials budget and develop a plan that allocates the budget to support current strategic goals.

1. Define the overall goals of project, i.e., reallocating budget to:
   a) Cover serials inflation.
   b) Provide funds for new electronic resources.
   c) Support new strategic directions of parent organization (e.g., outreach, programmatic shifts, emphasis on undergraduates, support local businesses' access to the Internet, etc.).
2. Identify the available resources including: staff time and expertise, funding, computers, and software. Locate peer libraries that may have completed similar projects that can be used as models.
3. Develop a realistic time line for assessment project.
4. Identify indirect (surrogate) information:
   a) User demographic information.

   b) Collection statistics including the number of titles, the age of titles, or the growth of collections.
   c) Circulation statistics by user group and subject.
   d) Use statistics including use of noncirculating collections such as periodicals or reference, as well as use of electronic resources.
   e) Marketplace information including the cost and availability of information resources.
   f) Strategic planning documents of the library and parent organization.
   g) Networking or consortial agreements.
   h) Document delivery program (subsidized or not).
   i) Alternative sources for information.
5. Conduct a baseline user satisfaction survey.
6. Develop a framework for assessment data. (E.g., will data be organized by LC class or some other subject organization? Will data be organized by user group? Will the data be organized in some other combination?)
7. Identify sources for the surrogate information and collect it.
8. Based upon the user demographic information, conduct a random survey of the identified user groups to determine directly from patrons their perceived information needs.
9. Input surrogate information and data gathered from survey in a relational database, spreadsheet, or statistical package.
10. Analyze data: Do you have the information you need to make the decisions required by the project? Does the data make sense?
11. Develop a plan to reallocate the budget.
12. At future intervals, test user satisfaction for impact.
13. Develop a time line to repeat the assessment so the budget allocation process can continue to be aligned with changing conditions.

C. Possible needs assessment for a school library/media center

The school district allocates annual funding for materials in the following fashion: a base amount is allocated to each library/media center and any additional funding must be requested and documented for specific needs. These needs may be due to a new curriculum area (e.g., foreign language courses), updating an existing area (e.g., geography or math), or changes in the demographics of the pupils and their families (e.g., a new population of immigrants who do not speak English).

1. Form a consulting group among teachers, colleagues in other school library/media centers, and volunteers from among the parents.
2. With the consulting group, discuss the needs, develop assumptions, and clarify requirements for justifying additional allocation. The consulting group also determines those types of data that are appropriate and could be collected. Establish the time line.
3. Determine available resources, staff time, and possible assistance from colleagues who may have experience with projects of this type.
4. Collect available surrogate data, including community demographics, number of students affected (including projections for the near future), and number of courses taught.
5. Hold focus groups or interview teachers not already involved to determine extent of information needed.
6. Conduct mini-assessment of the area of the collection involved. What additional resources are available and accessible from other libraries, including neighboring libraries? What alternative sources can be used, e.g., Internet and ILL?
7. If there are obsolete materials in the collection, identify need for weeding and establish timetable.
8. Search for appropriate, currently available materials in area of need.
9. With consulting group, analyze data collected, then review and prioritize a list of materials.
10. Compile a report with a list of necessary resources to submit for approval and funding.

D. Possible needs assessment for the addition of a new branch library

The main library system has been asked to provide library services to customers through a new site separate from the main library building. Funds have been allocated for the project. Now it is time to develop the information resources that need to be provided to the library's patrons.

1. Determine the goals of the assessment project and develop ideas about customers who might be served by the new facility and what information resources the users will need. Set a time line.
2. Consult the institutional strategic plans, reports, or planning documents that were developed by the parent organization as part of the process of designing and building the new branch.
3. Identify the internal resources that can be used for the assessment (staff time, computers, etc.)
4. Develop baseline data concerning the demographic outline of the customers to be served.
5. Hold focus groups with selected members of the identified user groups.
6. Interview several potential users to follow up on themes revealed in focus groups and to gather other pertinent information on goals for the new branch.
7. Analyze data from interviews and focus groups. Compare information on stated needs with initial library staff assumptions. Determine if there are other libraries with like missions and clienteles, and consult with them to determine if those libraries have any data such as circulation statistics or collection development policies that might prove useful. Prepare summary report to library and users.
8. Do a baseline study of currently available local resources. This would include collection statistics on print and journal holdings, access to electronic information, and access to document delivery services.
9. Develop a plan for supplying needs of the new branch program.

E. Possible needs assessment for consortial cooperation on serial subscriptions and document delivery

Suppose your library is a member of a group of libraries that plans to maximize access to serial information through the sharing of resources. Subscriptions to low-circulating journals will be reduced with individual members taking responsibility to maintain targeted subscriptions while others cut their subscriptions. Document delivery services will provide access to the journals for the group.

1. Review strategic documents related to the consortium in question.
2. Define goals of project: What areas need to be looked at? Are all subject areas included, and all serials to be reviewed, or only subsets?
3. Identify available resources (staff time, funding, computers and software) and determine if any peer libraries have completed similar projects that can be used as models.
4. Develop a realistic time line for assessment project.
5. Identify indirect (surrogate) information that needs to be gathered:
   a) List serial subscriptions, including costs for each member.
   b) Identify the overlap in serial subscription lists among consortium members. The easiest way to do this is to export a file containing, at minimum, title and ISSN from the local ILS of each member and load the file into a database management program.
   c) Gather circulation and in-house use statistics for all members.
   d) Analyze journal ISI impact factors for commonly held titles.
   e) Assemble collection development or collection service policies of all members.
6. Identify journal titles that could be purchased on a cooperative basis (i.e., not owned locally but by another consortium member).
7. Identify new titles that are not currently owned by anyone in the consortium.
8. Develop user survey to look at patrons' expectations concerning access to journals and document delivery. Survey should address specific needs concerning acceptable turnaround times.
9. Issue draft of plan to all library users for all members. Plan should include impact on specific titles. Solicit comments from users.
10. Complete database by adding surrogate information and specific comments from patrons.
11. Review all data and make proposal to consortium.

F. Possible preliminary needs assessment to assist development of statewide cooperative resource-sharing ventures in support of small public libraries

Suppose you are a member of a strategic planning committee sponsored by your state library and the state library association charged with determining future directions for statewide cooperative collection development efforts. There is a high proportion of rural public libraries in your state with one or two permanent staff. At one of several large annual meetings, there is an opportunity to do modified focus groups of staff from these small libraries.

1. Review with the committee the past requests to the state library and library association for support of small public libraries, previous planning documents, reports of cooperative collection development activities that focused on or included small libraries, etc. Review documents that define the current political environment for state libraries and any strategic plans that could impact future developments.
2. Have the committee identify potential questions to ask the focus groups. What does the committee need to know from this group?
3. Prioritize the list to reduce it to the most important three or four questions.
4. Plan the logistics for the focus groups. Select one of the annual meetings as a venue and designate someone to follow up with scheduling.
5. Identify and order necessary supplies (flip charts, 5-by-7-inch cards, markers, sticker dots for group voting, etc.)
6. Decide whether the groups will be taped and arrange for equipment if necessary.
7. Address the large gathering and explain why the committee needs input from small public libraries. Discuss some of the recent initiatives that have involved or assisted small libraries and give an overview of the current cooperative environment in the state. Go over the list of questions and the process that will take place in smaller groups. Ask if there are any questions from participants to help clarify the questions or the process. Make it clear to the participants that their honest opinions are highly valued. The participants' feedback should be what they really think, not what they think the library wants to hear.

8. Initiate the modified focus groups. Ask the participants to count off and separate into groups of no more than ten each. Ask for volunteers to moderate each group. Give the participants a list of questions and ask them to take a few minutes to write down ideas on 5-by-7-inch cards. Ask them to take turns and announce their ideas, which the moderator will write on the flip chart. Wander from group to group to facilitate. After all ideas are on the charts, encourage participants to ask each other questions or offer comments about the identified issues, and ask the moderator to record any further issues. Finally, give each member three sticker dots and ask them to prioritize the list by placing stickers on the flip chart next to the issues they think are the most important.

9. Bring the individual focus groups back together. Explain to them that this final session will be tape-recorded and ask them to help identify overall themes from flip charts. Ask for any comments on the priorities identified by the smaller groups. Encourage comments or further ideas.

10. Transcribe flip charts, 5-by-7-inch cards, and tapes made of the final session. Summarize themes and present to the committee for consideration when assessing planning priorities in support of small public libraries.

V. Pointers and pitfalls

When undertaking any complex project, there are always stumbling blocks. The assessment of library users' information needs is no different. There are several common errors that frequently occur. An assessment project will be more successful if the following suggestions are taken into consideration. The list is not inclusive of all that might go wrong; these are just the most frequent, common errors.

A. Avoid the easy-data-is-the-right-data syndrome

George Easton, former Baldrige Award inspector, notes that one of the most prevalent mistakes made by companies trying to initiate a data-driven decision model is that the companies use data that is easy to collect and then assume that this data is representative of user needs. For example, they might attach too much significance to circulating collection statistics as an indicator of user information needs instead of conducting the more rigorous and difficult study of user behavior that would include in-house use, use of document delivery services, use of other collections (personal, departmental, etc.), and electronic access. The smart approach to data gathering involves the identification and collection of data types that answer the crucial questions of the study rather than gathering together data that is readily at hand. The scope of the project needs to define the data types to be gathered (often by setting explicit criteria). If this data is too expensive or difficult to collect, then the scope of the project may have to be reexamined; but easily obtained data that does not address the needs of the project should not be substituted.

B. Do not confuse data types

It is not necessarily problematic to gather different types of data in one coordinated effort, but it is important to be clear that the data types are different when analyzed. The following are some examples that could lead to trouble:

1. Primary (direct information from patrons) and secondary (surrogate) data.
2. Surveys that ask users to both rank and rate items.
3. User satisfaction surveys with data gathering (user needs assessment) surveys.
4. Qualitative and quantitative data in the same question.
5. Data from focus groups and statistically representative data from surveys.

C. Do not confuse measurement units

A simple example would be mixing numbers of volumes with numbers of titles. Another is mixing FTE with head count when assessing user groups or mixing averages, medians, and modes when doing simple statistical summaries (especially with graphics).

D. The numbers sometimes do not tell the whole story

For most assessments it may not be possible to identify and quantify all important variables. Also, it may be difficult to identify the crucial independent variable. When the independent variable(s) change, the dependent variables reflect that change indicating a chain of causality is present. It is important to carefully analyze the overall validity of the data before using the data solely to develop outcomes. An example would be using a closed-ended question that asks patrons to rank current services. There may be a service that your patrons want that is not currently offered, and many users may feel the service is more important than those currently offered. If you were to develop priorities based solely on your data, you might miss the opportunity to improve your information resources.

E. Context is important

It is advisable in most cases to place the assessment results in the environmental context of the library and the parent organization, and rely on strategic information about potential future services, budgetary changes, etc. that are not reflected in user expression of needs.

F. Recognize under-represented groups

In any survey or assessment it is advisable to determine if some groups are not represented in the results. One way of determining this is to match known demographic data about the user population being surveyed with the results of questions on the survey designed to elicit the same demographic data. For example, if 20 percent of library users are over the age of fifty but the response rate from this subset is much less than this proportion, the sampling strategy may be flawed or this age group may represent a low-use population that needs to be reached in some other way. Another example would be a group whose primary language is not English, but the survey instrument is English-only. The absence of data from these groups undermines the effectiveness of assessments.

G. Recognize service impacts of the unknown user

Be aware that the sample may completely miss a potential user group with latent service impacts that are not yet recognized in your traditional user base. If a population is surveyed using local patron records, those users who make use of collections and other related services without registering as an official user may be missed. Or there may be a growing user group that accesses the collection electronically and will not be reached by in-house surveys or surveys directed at known users. Some library collections have broad appeal and support the intellectual and cultural life of a community, thus reflecting possible usage beyond that represented by primary user groups. The bottom line is that these groups can skew data that describes how information resources are being used. An example would be an unrecognized group outside the primary patron group, e.g., students from a local commercial educational institution that lacks library services or students in a distance learning situation using local resources for course support, heavily using a narrow set of materials. This use skews the data and may not reflect the true needs of the total primary patron population for those information resources that were used by the outside group.

Glossary

Access/Ownership Available information at the time of demand (just in time) = access; ownership = collection for archival or research purposes.

Accountability Monitoring, measuring, and evaluating the performance and progress of policies, plans, and programs to ensure they achieve the results intended.

Benchmarking The continuous process of collecting information on external standards, processes, and/or best practices. An organization can then compare itself to any national standards or superior performers to identify opportunities for improvement. Benchmarking can be useful at various points in the strategic planning process. It can be used to determine potential strengths, weaknesses, opportunities, and threats when conducting an internal/external assessment. Benchmarking can also support performance measurement. Quantifiable data derived from the benchmarking process can be used to set realistic performance targets for the future.

Cost-benefit analysis A management tool that involves calculating or estimating the known costs and potential benefits of a course of action under consideration.

Course-pack publishing Reading (and/or reserve) lists prepared by commercial copy services under the direction of the instructor and sold to students.

Customer satisfaction The focus of total quality management (TQM) techniques. It includes contribution to the fulfillment of the customer's goals for the use of information or materials; fulfillment of customer's specific wishes, needs, and expectations;

and customer anticipation that future needs will also be met. Customer satisfaction is measured by both qualitative and quantitative data.

Customers   People, internal or external to the organization, who receive or use what an organization produces. Customers are also those whose best interests are served by the actions of an organization. Customers can also be clients, or users of a service.

Effectiveness measure   From the effectiveness perspective, performance measurement incorporates a focus on outcomes. In contrast to efficiency (which maximizes outputs in relation to inputs), effectiveness strives to maximize outcomes in relation to inputs. Outcomes address the impact or benefit of a program in a broad sense which could include the social context.

Efficiency measures   A type of performance measure that reflects the cost of providing a good or service. Cost can be expressed in terms of dollars or time per unit of output (or outcome). Efficiency measures can also be expressed as a ratio of outputs to inputs. Efficiency strives to maximize outputs in relation to inputs.

Environmental scan   An analysis of key external elements or forces that influence the conditions under which an organization functions.

Evaluation   The systematic review of the missions, goals, objectives, action plans, performance measures, and operations of an organization or program.

External variables   Factors not controlled through the policy or program that may have independent and significant effects on outcomes such as economic downturns, population shifts, technological advances, and cultural differences or changes.

Gap analysis   An assessment of the difference between the present state and the desired future state.

Goals   The desired end result, generally after three or more years.

Inputs   A type of performance measure that identifies the amounts of resources needed to provide a particular product or service. Inputs include labor hours, materials, and equipment. Inputs can also represent demand factors, such as target populations.

Integrated information needs   Library users may need information in a variety of formats, singly or in combination. Services should be designed in an integrated manner, and needs assessments should cover the breadth of information options.

Internal/External assessment An analysis and evaluation of internal conditions and external factors that affect the organization.

Mission/Statement A short, comprehensive statement of purpose. The mission identifies what an agency, program, or subprogram does (or should do) and for whom it is done.

Nonusers Potential, but not current library users.

Objective Specific and measurable targets for accomplishment of a goal that are aggressive yet attainable, result-oriented, and time-bound, and must be accomplished in the stated time frame. Customer-focused objectives are designed to address satisfaction.

Operational plan An annual work plan. It indicates what portion of a strategic plan will be addressed by a program during an operational period.

Outcomes A type of performance measure that addresses the actual results achieved and the impact or benefit of a public program. Outcomes are derived from missions and goals. Customer-focused outcomes are used to evaluate quality of performance.

Outputs A type of performance measure that reflects the amount of goods and services produced by a program.

Performance accountability A means of judging policies and programs by measuring their progress toward achieving agreed-upon performance targets. Performance accountability systems are composed of three components: defining performance measures (including outcomes), measuring performance, and reporting results.

Performance measures A management tool that measures work performed and results achieved. Used to evaluate the effectiveness or quality of a process, service, or product.

Planning assumptions Expectations concerning future trends that could significantly impact performance (derived from the internal/external assessment results) that are used when developing the strategic plan.

Primary users User populations identified in the mission statement as those central groups to whom services are directed.

Quality measures A type of performance measure that represents effectiveness in meeting the expectations of customers and stakeholders. Quality measures may reflect reliability, accuracy, courtesy, competence, responsiveness, and completeness associated with a product or service. Feedback and continuous improvement should focus on quality as the primary measure of performance, demonstrating the focus on the customer.

Stakeholders   Organizations, groups, or individuals that have a vested interest or expect certain levels of performance or compliance from the organization. Stakeholders do not necessarily use the products or receive the services of a program. Sometimes referred to as expectation groups. May be internal or external to the organization.

Strategic impact   Impact of innovative/changed policy or procedure measured in relation to strategic issues. Focus on strategic impact is directed toward achieving the goals and directives of the strategic plan.

Strategic issues   Those concerns of vital importance to the organization. They often impact several or all of the programs in an agency. Identifying these few crucial concerns can help an agency focus on high-priority goals for the organization as a whole.

Strategic plan   A practical action-oriented guide based on an examination of internal and external factors, which directs goal setting and resource allocation to achieve meaningful results over time.

Surrogate data (Also secondary information or data)   This type of data is indirectly representative of use patterns. There is no direct correlation between surrogate data and actual use of information by library patrons, but it is often useful in informing decision-making processes as it does describe the current environment at a macro level and is especially effective when used in conjunction with a broader spectrum of data. Surrogate data is very useful in defining the current environment and the demographic characteristics of the user base. It does not describe actual needs or the library patrons' use of information resources.

SWOT analysis   An abbreviation used to denote an analysis of an organization's *strengths, weaknesses, opportunities,* and *threats.* The SWOT analysis is part of the internal/external assessment an organization conducts to analyze and evaluate internal conditions (strengths and weaknesses) and external factors (opportunities and threats) that affect the organization.

Total quality management (TQM)   An integrated management methodology that aligns the activities of all employees in an organization with the common focus of customer satisfaction through continuous improvement in the quality of all activities, goods, and services.

Trend A broad, historical direction in behavior, perceptions, and values.

Values Core beliefs, principles, and philosophies describing how an organization conducts itself.

Variables Controllable or uncontrollable factors that may affect policy, planning, or program outcomes.

Vision A compelling conceptual image of the desired future. A vision focuses and ennobles an idea about a future state of being in such a way as to excite and compel an organization toward its attainment. It crystallizes what management wants the organization to be in the future.

Bibliography

Adams, Mignon S., and Jeffrey A. Beck. *User Surveys in College Libraries.* Clip Note No. 23. Chicago: American Library Association, 1995.

Answering Questions: Methodology for Determining Cognitive and Communicative Processes in Survey Research. Eds. Norbert Schwartz and Seymour Sudman. San Francisco: Jossey-Bass, 1996.

Backman, Dan, and Jeffrey Rubin. "Web Log Analysis: Finding a Recipe for Success." *Network Computing*, vol. 8, no 11 (June 15, 1997): 87–94.

Bahde, Wanda Johnston. "User Satisfaction: How We Measured It." *Community & Junior College Libraries*, vol. 9, no. 1 (1999): 57–67.

Bejou, David, et al. "A Critical Incident Approach to Examining the Effects of Service Failures on Customer Satisfaction." *Journal of Travel Research*, vol. 35, no. 1 (summer 1996): 37–43.

Berger, Kenneth W., and Richard W. Hines. "What Does the User Really Want? The Library User Survey Project at Duke University." *Journal of Academic Librarianship*, vol. 20, no. 5–6 (November 1994): 306–10.

Bishop, Ann Peterson, and Cliff Bishop. "The Policy Role of User Studies." *Serials Review*, vol. 21, no. 1 (spring 1995): 17–26.

Bitner, Mary Jo, et al. "The Service Encounter." *Journal of Marketing*, vol. 54, no. 1 (January 1990): 71.

Buchanan, Robert W., Charles Lukaszewski, and Robert W. Buchanan, Jr. *Measuring the Impact of Your Web Site.* New York: John Wiley & Sons, 1997.

Carrico, Steven B. "The Cost-Effectiveness of Serial Exchanges at the University of Florida Library." *Serials Review*, vol. 23, no. 1 (spring 1997): 23–32.

Carrigan, Dennis P. "Data-Guided Collection Development: A Promise Unfulfilled." *College & Research Libraries*, vol. 57, no. 5 (September 1996): 429–38.

Chressanthis, George A., et al. "The Determinants of Library Subscription Prices of the Top-Ranked Economics Journals." *Journal of Economic Education*, vol. 25, no. 3 (fall 1994): 367–84.

Clougherty, Leo., John W. Forys, and Toby Lyles. "The University of Iowa Libraries' Undergraduate User Needs Assessment." *College & Research Libraries*, vol. 59, no. 6 (November 1998): 572–84.

Crispell, Diane. "Drawing the Line." *American Demographics*, vol. 18, no. 7 (July 1996): 2.

Crist, Margo, et al. "User Studies." *Wilson Library Bulletin*, vol. 68, no. 6 (February 1994): 38–42.

Demographics (a directory). *American Demographics*, vol. 18, no. 9 (September 1996): 9.

Easton, George S. "A Baldrige Examiner's Assessment of U.S. Total Quality Management." In *The Death and Life of the American Quality Movement*, ed. Robert E. Cole, 11–41. New York: Oxford University Press, 1995.

Fowler, Floyd J. *Survey Research Methods*. Newberry Park, Calif.: Sage Publications, 1993.

Francis, Jim. "Allocating Resources towards the Complete Library." *Australian Public Libraries and Information Services*, vol. 9, no. 3–4 (September/December 1996): 147–56.

Fuegi, D. "Towards a National Standard for a Public Library User Survey." *Public Library Journal-Public Libraries Group*, vol. 9, no. 2 (1994): 49.

Fukuyama, Mary A. "Critical Incidents in Multicultural Counseling Supervision: A Phenomenological Approach." *Counselor Education & Supervision*, vol. 34, no. 2 (December 1994): 142–52.

Goodman, John A., Scott M. Broetzmann, and Colin Adamson. "Ineffective—That's the Problem with Customer Satisfaction Surveys." *Quality Progress*, vol. 25 (May 1992): 35–38.

Guide to the Evaluation of Library Collections. Ed. Barbara Lockett. Collection Management & Development Committee, Resources Section, Resources and Technical Services Division, American Library Association, 1989.

Hafner, Arthur W. *Descriptive Statistical Techniques for Librarians*. 2d ed. Chicago: American Library Association, 1997.

Hawbaker, A. Craig, and Cynthia K. Wagner. "Periodical Ownership Versus Fulltext Online Access: A Cost-Benefit Analysis." *Journal of Academic Librarianship*, vol. 22, no. 2 (March 1996): 105–10.

Hernon, Peter. *Statistics: A Component of the Research Process*. Norwood, N.J.: Ablex, 1991.

Herzog, Kate, et al. "Designing Effective Journal Use Studies." *Serials Librarian*, vol. 24, no. 3–4 (1994): 189–93.

Kerslake, Evelyn, and Anne Goulding. "Focus Groups: Their Use in LIS Research Data Collection." *Education for Information,* vol. 14, no. 3 (October 1996): 225–33.

Kleiner, Janellyn Pickering, and Charles Hamaker. "Libraries 2000: Transforming Libraries Using Document Delivery, Needs Assessment, and Networked Resources—Three Projects at Louisiana State University." *College & Research Libraries,* vol. 58 (July 1997): 355–74.

Kreuger, Richard A. *Focus Groups: A Practical Guide for Applied Research.* 2d ed. Thousand Oaks, Calif.: Sage Publications, 1994.

Kuhlthau, Carol. "Inside the Search Process: Information Seeking from the User's Perspective." *Journal of the American Society for Information Science,* vol. 42 (June 1991): 361–71.

LaGuardia, Cheryl, and Joseph Boisse. "User Needs, Library Mandates, and Information Magic." *Online,* vol. 18, no. 3 (May 1994): 9–12.

Laughingly, John H. and William A. Schiemann. "From Balanced Scorecard to Strategic Gauges: Is Measurement Worth It?" *Management Review,* vol. 85, no. 3 (March 1996): 56–62.

Luborsky, Mark R., and Robert L. Rubinstein. "Sampling in Qualitative Research: Rationale, Issue, and Methods." *Research on Aging,* vol. 17, no. 1 (March 1995): 89–114.

Managing for Results: Strategic Planning and Performance Measurement Handbook. Governor's Office of Strategic Planning and Budgeting, Governor's Office for Excellence in Government. Phoenix: State of Arizona, 1995.

Martin, Laurence L., and Peter M. Kettner. *Measuring the Performance of Human Service Programs.* Thousand Oaks, Calif.: Sage, 1996.

McCandless, Patricia, et al. *The Invisible User: User Needs Assessment for Library Public Services.* Washington, D.C.: Office of Management Studies, Association of Research Libraries, 1985.

McClure, Charles R., et al. "Assessing the Academic Networked Environment." *Journal of Academic Librarianship,* vol. 22, no. 4 (July 1996): 285–90.

McClure, Charles R., and Peter Hernon. *Library and Information Science Research: Perspectives and Strategies for Improvement.* Norwood, N.J.: Ablex Pub. Corp., c1991.

McClure, Charles R. "User-based Data Collection Techniques and Strategies for Evaluating Networked Information Services." *Library Trends,* vol. 42, no. 4 (spring 1994): 591–608.

Mirani, Rajesh, and William R. King. "Impacts of End-User and Information Center Characteristics on End-User Computing Support." *Journal of Management Information Systems,* vol. 11, no. 1 (summer 1994): 141–67.

Murray, J., T. Huynh, and K. Williamson. "A Needs-Analysis Survey of Users of an Audio Book Library." *Journal of Visual Impairment and Blindness*, vol. 89, no. 2 (1995): 161.

Naylor, Maiken. "A Comparison of Two Methodologies for Counting Current Periodical Use." *Serials Review*, vol. 19, no. 1 (spring 1993): 27–34.

Norman, O. Gene. "The Impact of Electronic Information Sources on Collection Development: A Survey of Current Practice." *Library Hi Tech*, vol. 15, no. 1–2 (1997): 123–33.

Oppermann, Martin. "E-Mail Surveys: Potentials and Pitfalls." *Marketing Research*. vol. 7 (summer 1995): 29–33.

"PC Week Navigator" (log analysis tools). *PC Week*, vol. 13, no. 42 (October 21, 1996): 64.

Powell, Alan. "Management Models and Measurement in the Virtual Library." *Special Libraries*, vol. 85, no. 4 (fall 1994): 260–64.

Rogers, Michael. "New Jersey Library Analyzes Community." *Library Journal*, vol. 117, no. 17 (October 1, 1992): 18

Saleem, Naveed. "An Empirical Test of the Contingency Approach to User Participation in Information Systems." *Journal of Management Information Systems*, vol. 13, no. 1 (summer 1996): 145–67.

Schmidt, Diane, et al. "Biology Journal Use at an Academic Library: A Comparison of Use Studies." *Serials Review*, vol. 20, no. 2 (summer 1994): 45–63.

Successful Focus Groups: Advancing the State of the Art. Ed. David L. Morgan. Newbury Park, Calif.: Sage Publications, 1993.

The Survey Kit. Thousand Oaks, Calif.: Sage Publications, 1995.

Talbot, Dawn E., Gerald R. Lowell, and Kerry Martin. "From the Users' Perspective—The UCSD Libraries User Survey Project." *Journal of Academic Librarianship*, vol. 24, no. 5 (September 1998): 357–65.

Tian, Jie, and Sharon Wiles-Young. "The Convergence of User Needs, Collection Building, and the Electronic Publishing Market Place." *Serials Librarian*, vol. 38, no. 3/4 (2000): 333–40.

User Surveys in ARL Libraries. Ed. Elaine Brekke and Laura Center. Washington, D.C.: Association of Research Libraries, Office of Management Services, 1995. SPEC Kit 205.

Viswesvaran, Chockalingam, et al. "How Definitive Are Conclusions Based on Survey Data: Estimating Robustness to Nonresponse." *Personnel Psychology*, vol. 46, no. 3 (autumn 1993): 551–68.

Waite, Charles A. "The Statistics Corner: Update on Census Bureau Economic Data Programs." *Business Economics*, vol. 29, no. 3 (July 1994): 66–70.

Walden, Graham R. "Selected Reference Sources in Polling and Survey Research Methodology, 1971–1996." *Reference Services Review* (winter 1996): 49–66.

Weaver, Patricia. "A Student-Centered, Classroom-Based Approach to Collection Building." *Journal of Academic Librarianship*, vol. 25, no. 3 (May 1999): 202–11.

"WebTrends Goes National." *State Government News*, vol. 38, no. 9 (September 1995): 16.

Weingand, Darlene E. *Customer Service Excellence: A Concise Guide for Librarians.* Chicago: ALA, 1997.

Weingart, Sandra J., and Janet A. Anderson. "When Questions Are Answers: Using a Survey to Achieve Faculty Awareness of the Library's..." *College & Research Libraries*, vol. 61, no. 2 (March 2000): 127–35.

Westbrook, Lynn. "User Needs: A Synthesis and Analysis of Current Theories for the Practitioner." *RQ*, vol. 32, no. 4 (summer 1993): 541–600.

Whitlatch, Jo Bell. "Unobtrusive Studies and the Quality of Academic Library Reference Services." *College & Research Libraries*, vol. 50 (March 1989): 181–94.

Williamson, Kirsty. "The Role of Research in Professional Practice: With Reference to the Assessment of the Information and Library Needs of Older People." *Australasian Public Libraries and Information Services*, vol. 12, no 4 (Dec. 1999): 145–53.

Zhang, W. "Assessing Users' Information Needs, Expectations and Quality of Services: Olin Library User Survey." *Journal of Educational Media and Library Sciences*, vol. 33, no. 4 (1996): 369.

Zhao, Dian G. "Usage Statistics Collection and Management in the ELINOR Electronic Library." *Journal of Information Science*, vol. 21, no. 1 (1995): 1–10.

Zollars, Cheryl. "The Perils of Periodical Indexes: Some Problems in Constructing Samples for Content Analysis." *Communication Research*, vol. 21, no. 6 (December 1994): 698–717.

World Wide Web Resources

The Brown University Library User Needs Team
A site that describes the activities of this group
http://www.brown.edu/Facilities/University_Library/MODEL/lunt/index.html

Campbell Development Surveys Homepage!
Campbell Development Surveys form an integrated battery of measurement instruments designed to provide diagnostic information about individuals, work groups, and organizations.
http://www.ncs.com/assessments/tests/campbell.htm

Columbia's Online Books Evaluation Project
This project employed a wide variety of tools—including server data; a variety of online, mailed, and hand-distributed surveys; and individual and group interviews—that are described in detail in the project research plan and final report.
http://www.columbia.edu/cu/libraries/digital/texts/about.html

Community Needs Assessment Study
A how-to site that describes approaches to conducting community needs assessments for public libraries.
http://www.lib.az.us/cdt/commneeds.htm

Graphics, Visualization, and Usability Center at Georgia Tech
Samples of online Web surveys.
http://www.cc.gatech.edu/gvu/user_surveys/

HyperLib Deliverable 1.2
In-depth survey of OPAC-usage hypertext interfaces to library information systems. University of Antwerp-University of Loughborough.
http://www.ua.ac.be/MAN/WP12/root.html

International Coalition of Library Consortia (ICOLC)
Guidelines for statistical measures of usage of Web-based, indexed, abstracted, and full-text resources. Describes a set of guidelines for statistical measures for assessing use of electronic resources.
http://www.library.yale.edu/consortia/webstats.html

Log Analysis Tools
Brief descriptions and links to log-analysis software packages. Provided by Yahoo!, this site is not by any means inclusive of all software for log analysis. Many of the programs are available free on the Web.
http://www.yahoo.com/Computers_and_Internet/Software/ Internet/World_Wide_Web/Servers/Log_Analysis_Tools/

Mail List Discussion—Surveying User Needs: Do We Really Want to Know?
CRISTAL-ED (Coalition on Reinventing Information Science, Technology, and Library Education). Funding by Kellogg; University of Michigan, School of Information.
http://www.si.umich.edu/cristaled/postings/V35.html

Needs Assessment Program
Describes the needs assessment program conducted at the University of Tennessee-Knoxville Libraries, 1993-1994.
http://www.lib.utk.edu/~plan/needs/index.html

Research Methods Knowledge Base
According to site developer William M. Trochim, "the Research Methods Knowledge Base is a comprehensive Web-based textbook that addresses all of the topics in a typical introductory undergraduate or graduate course in social research methods."
http://trochim.human.cornell.edu/kb/

The Survey Center
The Survey Center provides business-to-business marketing research services. It has the ability to manage research projects from conception to completion and offers project support services.
http://www.thesurveycenter.com

SURVEYNET
Progressive Computer Services—online, interactive, user-programmable survey engine capable of collecting a wide variety of information and demographics.
http://www.survey.net/

UIUC Library User Survey & Needs Assessment Spring 1998 Summary
Summary of a user survey conducted at the University of Illinois Library in the spring of 1998.
http://www.library.uiuc.edu/collections/a-survey.htm

University of Iowa Libraries User Needs Assessment Group
A summary of the surveys conducted by this group in 1998.
http://www.lib.uiowa.edu/lib/unag/

User Needs Assessment Berkeley Digital Library Project
A brief overview of the Berkeley project by Nancy A. Van House and links to related papers.
http://elib.cs.berkeley.edu/user-needs.html

User-Study Related Material
A selection of links to documents on the Web, retrieved by using some of its major search tools. Target groups: Librarians, students, and researchers in the field of library and information science. Sections: Theory and background, methodology, surveys, and e-conferences.
http://www.ub2.lu.se/~biblutb/proj4/Userstrukt.html#Theory

Vancouver Island Regional Library Market Survey 1996
Purpose, methods, and results of a survey of Vancouver Island Regional Library users.
http://www.virl.bc.ca/graphics/about/survey.htm

WebTrends

A comprehensive software system that compiles and analyzes Web-site usage information.

http://www.webtrends.com/products/default.htm

Dora Biblarz
Associate Dean—TQS/Continuous Improvement
Arizona State University

Stephen Bosch
Information Access Librarian
University of Arizona

Chris Sugnet
Assistant Director for Collections
University of Nevada, Las Vegas

Guide Developed for:
American Library Association
Association for Library Collections & Technical Services
Collection Management and Development Section
Collection Development Issues for the Practitioner Committee